Land *of* Dreams

A History
in Photographs
of the
British Columbia
Interior

MEREDITH BAIN
WOODWARD

Land *of* Dreams

A History
in Photographs
of the
British Columbia
Interior

Altitude Publishing
Banff and Vancouver

Front cover: The sternwheeler *Hazelton* navigates the current of the Skeena River at Ringbolt Island. Launched in 1901, the *Hazelton* was one of several vessels that served Skeena River communities until the Grand Trunk Pacific Railway was completed in 1914.

Back cover: A young prospector pulls supplies up the Kootenay River in 1902. In undeveloped areas of the province, waterways provided important transportation corridors.

Page 1: These outdoor enthusiasts relax after a successful day of duck hunting at Gus Adams' camping outfit near Kaslo, ca. 1895.

Page 2: The Kettle Valley Railway ran from Midway to Hope (1916-1962), linking the towns of the southern Interior. The 480 kilometres of track climbed from 340 to 1240 metres above sea level and travelled over 18 trestle bridges, such as this one at Canyon Creek.

Page 5: These Kutenai teepees were photographed near Invermere in 1922.

Canadian Cataloguing in Publication Data
Woodward, Meredith Bain, 1944–
Land of Dreams:
A History in Photographs of the British Columbia Interior
ISBN 0-919381-22-7
1. British Columbia – History – Pictorial works.
I. Woodward, Ron, 1944– II. Title.
FC3812.W66 1993
971.1'0022'2
C93-091032-X
F1087.8.W66 1993

Photo editor: Ron Woodward
Editor: Maureen Nicholson
Design: Robert MacDonald, MediaClones Inc.

Made in Western Canada
Printed and bound in Western Canada by Friesen Printers, Altona Manitoba, using Canadian-made paper and vegetable-based inks.

This book was published with the assistance of the Department of Communications, Book Publishing Industry Development Program.

Altitude GreenTree Program
Altitude will plant in Western Canada twice as many trees as were used in the manufacturing of this book.

Acknowledgments
The author gratefully acknowledges the assistance of the following people: Anna Payawal, Laurie Robertson, Andrea Smith, Marius Wolfe, and Amber Woodward.

Altitude Publishing Canada Ltd.

Box 490, Banff Alberta T0L 0C0

402 West Pender Street, Suite 512
Vancouver BC V6B 1T6

Contents

An Uncharted Wilderness

In the 1700s, explorers from Spain, Great Britain, and Russia sailed the Pacific Coast of North America, dreaming of a "Northwest Passage" connecting the Atlantic and Pacific oceans. Although the route eluded them, they were rewarded instead by the abundant sea otter that proved to be a valuable trading commodity.

Despite the riches of the sea, the newcomers were not interested in settling in the rugged country now known as British Columbia. The barriers presented by the coastal mountains on the west and the Rocky Mountains on the east created a discouraging obstacle to such settlement. It seemed a land of wild rivers and cold mountain peaks – inhospitable and uninhabitable.

In fact, nearly 100,000 people lived in the area now known as British Columbia during that time, approximately 35,000 of them in the Interior. This indigenous population included a variety of language groups and social organizations based on political, religious, and cultural diversity developed over centuries. Some anthropologists say that Native people may have lived in the region as early as 40,000 years ago, before the last Ice Age. Artifacts found at Charlie Lake near present-day Fort St. John confirm Native settlement there about 11,000 years ago.

Our pictorial history of BC's Interior begins in 1793, a time of fierce competition for expanded territory among fur-trading companies. The British-based Hudson's Bay Company, established in 1670, had long held a monopoly on the fur trade in Canada. In the 1770s, a group of independent traders challenged this domination and formed the North West Company, headquartered in Montreal. The new group had to establish its own trading territories, however, and the search led them farther and farther west.

When Nor'Wester Alexander Mackenzie crossed the Rocky Mountains via the Peace River in 1793, he was looking for "the Great White River" described by Native people, an inland water route to the Pacific Ocean that would provide a cheaper and faster method of transporting furs and supplies to the East. Robert Gray, an American, had explored the mouth of the Columbia River in 1792.

Opposite: Although the territory west of the Rocky Mountains seemed an inhospitable wilderness to early fur traders, it supported an estimated population of 100,000 in 1800. While Interior tribes tended to be nomadic, an abundant supply of salmon and cedar allowed coastal Natives to develop permanent settlements and sophisticated artistic skills, such as pole carving. This cedar pole, photographed at Kitwancool in 1950, is of the Tsimshian people, whose territory extended almost to Fort George in the Interior.

Top: For part of his journey to the Pacific, Mackenzie travelled along Native "grease trails." Tsimshian caught the abundant oolichan – here pictured drying on racks – in the Nass River. The oil rendered became a valuable trading commodity, transported to the Interior over "grease trails." Because of their high oil content, the fish could be lit, and thus were also known as "candle fish."

Left: Scottish-born Alexander Mackenzie began his career as a fur trader while still a teenager. A charming man with a dogged determination and strong leadership qualities, he explored both the Mackenzie and Fraser rivers while searching for the Columbia. He was one of the few explorers to achieve recognition in his lifetime.

Far left: Although he had intended to follow the Fraser River to its mouth, Mackenzie was dissuaded by Native guides and a diminishing food supply. Accompanied by his party of nine, he reached the Pacific via the Blackwater River. His painted message marked one of the greatest exploration voyages in North American history.

Many then felt that the Columbia was the mythical river of Native legend and that control of the waterway meant control of the northwest fur trade.

On discovering the mighty and muddy river we now know as the Fraser, Mackenzie thought he had found the Columbia and planned to follow it to the Pacific Ocean. Familiar with what lay ahead, Mackenzie's Native interpreter "shed tears on the reflection of those dangers which we might encounter in our expedition." Convinced, Mackenzie abandoned his plan at what was later to become Fort Alexandria. Travelling over "grease" trails used as Native trade routes, he arrived at the village of Bella Coola in 1793, the first European to cross the continent north of Mexico.

Despite Mackenzie's achievement, the notion of the area as an inhospitable

Top: After a long and bitter rivalry, the Hudson's Bay Company and the North West Company amalgamated in 1821. Sir George Simpson, chief factor of the new company, visited all posts west of the Rockies in 1824 to determine whether their continuation was viable. His visit to Fort St. James was reenacted in 1924.

Right: Simon Fraser's career began with the North West Company in 1792 when he was 16 years old. In 1805, ordered to find the Natives' "Great White River," he crossed the Rocky Mountains, naming the area he found New Caledonia.

Far right: Regarded by some historians as the most important North West Company post in New Caledonia, Fort St. James was established in 1806 on Stuart Lake by Simon Fraser. It was here Daniel Harmon cultivated the first crops in the Interior.

wilderness persisted. Twelve years would pass before other traders followed.

Simon Fraser, also a member of the North West Company, continued Mackenzie's search in 1805. "I have been for a long period among the Rocky Mountains," he wrote of his exploration of the Fraser River, "but never have seen anything to equal this country, for I cannot find words to describe our situation at times ... The navigation was absolutely impracticable ... We were often in imminent danger."

Fraser named the land west of the Rockies New Caledonia in honour of his native Scotland. Between 1805 and 1808, he built the region's first fur-trading posts, among them Fort McLeod, Fort St. James, and Fort George (later to become Prince George). In 1808, determined to succeed where Mackenzie

Top: Fur traders relied heavily on Natives for a variety of services. Here Carrier Natives pack goods into the original Fort St. James during the 1924 centenary of Sir George Simpson's visit. The Carrier were so named because it was the custom of widows to carry the bones of their dead husbands on their backs during mourning.

Bottom: These chiefs, at Fort St. James in 1924, are wearing the distinctive Chilkat blankets, woven from the inner bark of cedar and mountain goat wool. Although the Tsimshian are believed to have originated the blankets, it was the Tlingits to the north who produced the coveted pieces on a large scale. Highly valued as a trading commodity, each blanket took about one year to weave.

had failed, Fraser travelled the treacherous, muddy river to its mouth, enduring numerous hardships along the way. He was bitterly disappointed to discover that he was at a point several degrees north of the latitude of the mouth of the Columbia – the "Great White River" had eluded Simon Fraser as well.

It was Fraser's colleague and contemporary, David Thompson, who finally charted the Columbia River. Between 1804 and 1806, Lewis and Clark had led a trailblazing expedition through the American West. As news spread, the Nor'Westers became worried about increased competition and more determined to find the Columbia River.

In 1807, accompanied by his young Métis wife and their three children, Thompson crossed the Rocky Mountains through Howse Pass near Golden. He built Kootenae House near present-day Invermere, the first fur-trading fort in the south-eastern Interior. Thompson then spent several years charting and exploring the Columbia system, estab-lishing forts in Idaho, Montana, and Washing-ton.

In the meantime, the Nor'Westers learned that American John Jacob Astor had sent a contingent of his

Pacific Fur Company traders to establish a fort at the mouth of the Colum-bia. They anxiously urged Thompson to continue to the coast.

When he arrived at the Pacific in 1811, he was too late. The Pacific Fur Company traders, busy building Fort Astoria, had arrived a few weeks before.

The next year, David Stuart of the Pacific Fur Company led an expedition north through the Okanagan Valley from Fort Astoria and established Fort Kamloops on the

Above: The marine fur trade in the northwest was largely based on the pelts of animals such as sea otters, sea lions, and seals. The exploration of New Caledonia added highly valued beaver and other fur to the traders' inventory. This Nishga'a chief likely hunted mountain goat, deer, and bear.

Thompson River, noting "the country is everywhere rich in furs, and the Natives very peaceable." However, that same year the Pacific Fur Company collapsed, and the North West Company gained control of the fur trade north of the Columbia River.

Times were changing for the fur companies. In 1821, as a survival measure, the Hudson's Bay and the North West companies merged as the Hudson's Bay Company. Using the Columbia River as a transportation route to its forts on the Pacific Coast, the HBC established fur brigade routes from Fort Alexandria on the Fraser River via Fort Kamloops and the Okanagan Valley. The traders stopped at way stations near the modern communities of Kelowna and Osoyoos.

Despite the collapse of the Pacific Fur Company, the Hudson's Bay Company was constantly wary of American encroachment of its western territory. The north-south corridors formed naturally by Interior geography encouraged transportation and communication links with the United States. This fear of economic and political domination from the south was to affect much of BC's subsequent development.

To protect its supply routes, the company built Fort Langley in the Fraser Valley in 1827 and Fort Victoria on Vancouver Island in 1843. In 1846, the Oregon Treaty defined the disputed border between the US and New Caledonia as the 49th parallel. In order to further protect its interests, the HBC created fur brigade trails entirely within its own territory that ran from Fort Kamloops through the Coquihalla Range of the Cascade Mountains. The company also built new forts at Yale and Hope.

Although fur-trading posts were the first non-Native settlements in New Caledonia, the companies did not encourage homesteaders, other entrepreneurs, or the growth of villages and towns. So complete was their notion of themselves as sojourners rather than settlers that many traders relied heavily on imported food supplies. An exception was trader Daniel Harmon, who grew his own grains and

Opposite: "We arrived at the first village of the Ackinroe nation," Simon Fraser wrote on June 28, 1808, "where we were received with as much kindness as if we had been their lost relations. Neat mats were spread for our reception, and plenty of salmon served in wooden dishes was placed before us." Salmon was a staple for many Native tribes. This early photograph shows fish-drying racks in the Fraser Canyon near Yale.

Above: In the 1700s, five tribes with about 10,000 people lived in the southern Interior. The Kutenai, one of three language groups of Interior Natives, were based in the southeastern Interior. Because the distinctive shapes of Kutenai canoes are similar to those of indigenous Siberian people, anthropologists have suggested an early link between the groups.

Right: Between 1959 and 1961, the Milliken excavation near Yale in the Fraser Canyon revealed human habitation seven to nine thousand years ago. The archeologists' discovery of charred cherry pits helped them date the settlement. Described as *i yem*, this site was a "lucky place" for catching salmon.

Top: North West Company trader David Thompson was successful in his search for the Columbia. He crossed the Rocky Mountains in 1807, building Kootenae House near present-day Invermere. This replica was built in 1922.

Bottom: Interior of Kootenae House. Despite David Thompson's major contribution to the exploration of New Caledonia, little evidence remains of his sojourn in the Columbia Valley. The replica of Kootenae House has since burned down and there are no known likenesses of Thompson.

Above: Evidence suggests that the Kutenai were originally Plains people, driven west by the Blackfoot in the 1700s. Indeed, the Kutenai crossed the Rockies to hunt buffalo two to three times a year and many of their customs were Plains-based. The *travois* pulled by this Kutenai woman was a sled-like apparatus used for transportation, an important piece of equipment for a nomadic people.

Right: In 1828, James Douglas was a young Hudson's Bay Company trader at Fort St. James. When he retired in 1864, he was governor of the colonies of Vancouver Island and British Columbia, having shaped much of the early development of the province.

vegetables at Fort St. James as early as 1806. He is credited with being New Caledonia's first farmer.

Like David Thompson, many traders partnered with Native or Métis women and raised families. Although the popular notion at the time was that such liaisons were not permanent, there were exceptions. Trader James Douglas married his Métis companion while at Fort St. James. Reflecting on the isolated life of the HBC fur trader, Douglas wrote, "The vapid monotony of an inland trading Post would be perfectly insufferable [except for] the many tender ties, which find a way to the heart."

Douglas became chief factor of the HBC and eventually governor of the new colonies of Vancouver Island and British Columbia. Although his wife remained very much in the background after Douglas became governor, Amelia Connolly Douglas was his lifelong companion. (Ironically, although Douglas' marriage to Connolly was frowned upon by Fort Victoria's "society," Douglas was

himself part West Indian.)

Many historians have described the relationship between Natives and fur traders as mutually beneficial, characterized by healthy interdependence. Although there was conflict from time to time, no large-scale incidents of violence and bloodshed are recorded.

However, it is undeniable that the introduction of trading goods such as iron tools and guns irrevocably changed the Natives' traditional way of life. And it is well documented that the introduction of whisky, Christianity, and disease took a devastating toll.

Residents of the posts, along with the occasional missionary, were virtually the only Europeans living in the Interior until the 1850s. Then – as if making up for lost time – pandemonium!

Above: Several early fur-trading posts became major settlements in the Interior. Fort Kamloops, established in 1812 by David Stuart of the Pacific Fur Company, is pictured here in 1865.

Opposite: For convenience in shipping, furs were pressed into 80-pound bundles – a pack-horse load. It was felt that bundling the furs minimized losses when crossing rivers. This press, at least 50 years old, was still in use at Fort St. John when it was photographed in 1915.

Gold!

Throughout history, gold has had a bewitching effect, holding promises of wealth and power for men and women around the globe.

In 1849, thousands of dreamers flocked to California searching for gold, a better life, a fulfillment of hopes and desires – El Dorado. As the California fields played out, the miners began looking elsewhere, some heading north to New Caledonia. Although a few found gold in the Thompson River near Kamloops in the early 1850s, the Hudson's Bay Company wanted to protect its fur-trading territory and kept the news quiet. However, in 1858, the HBC factor at Kamloops reluctantly sent samples south to San Francisco for assay, and word quickly spread.

Young James Hill was one of those itinerant California searchers who headed north. On March 23, 1858, about to give up his scrutiny of a sandy bar south of Yale in the Fraser River, his eye caught a glitter in the gravel. That glitter (spotted on Hill's 26th birthday) yielded two million dollars of placer gold in one season. The Fraser River Gold Rush was on.

Over the next few months between ten and twenty thousand prospectors came searching for El Dorado in New Caledonia. "Never in the history of the migrations of man has been seen a 'rush' so sudden and so vast," wrote Lillooet clergyman R.C. Lunden Brown in 1858.

Although some semblance of community was created

Above: The town of Hope was a faltering Hudson's Bay Company post in 1849. A decade later when this picture was taken, between ten and twenty thousand prospectors panned for gold nearby on the Fraser River, and eight paddlewheelers regularly docked here, transporting miners and supplies from the coast.

Chinamen Washing Gold Fraser River Canyon, B. C.

with the building of churches and businesses in settlements such as Yale and Hope, the mining towns were still wide-open, filled with goldseekers willing to celebrate their successes or drown their sorrows in the 24-hour saloons. Early missionary Reverend John Booth Good described Lytton as "a town which cannot be surpassed ... [for] ungodliness, profanity and vice."

The nomadic nature of these new residents concerned Governor James Douglas. They had little allegiance to country or community. Many of the miners were desperate, having cashed in their worldly possessions, leaving behind family and friends for one last chance at success.

Most of the miners in New Caledonia were American. Their presence not only could lead to a repeat of the desperado style of the American West, but it also might mean American domination of the territory as in Oregon.

Acting quickly, Governor Douglas shrewdly implemented licensing fees and regulations that established British sovereignty by default. He appointed 10 gold commissioners to collect taxes and oversee mining activity throughout the mainland and island colonies. He asked for and received a contingent of Royal Engineers from Britain. Although primarily road builders, the uniformed presence of the "sappers"

Above: The prospectors were an international group, many Chinese among them. Once the diggings on the lower Fraser River began to dwindle in 1859, many miners moved north and east to pursue possibilities in the Cariboo and Similkameen. Often Chinese miners such as these stayed behind to successfully work abandoned claims.

Opposite top: Yale was the head of navigation for the lower Fraser River. Passengers travelled this far on sternwheelers from the coast, but then continued on foot over precarious Native paths up the Fraser Canyon or over old fur brigade trails to the Cariboo goldfields. This photograph was taken in 1865, the year the Cariboo Wagon Road was completed.

Opposite bottom: Dubbed the "hanging judge," Matthew Baillie Begbie was 39 when he arrived from England in 1858. "Able, active, energetic, and highly talented, Mr. Begbie is a most valuable public servant. I feel greatly indebted to him," wrote Governor James Douglas. In recognition of his contributions, the judge was knighted in 1875 by Queen Victoria.

added identifiable authority to a land that before had none. And on August 2, 1858, as a result of Douglas' petition, Britain declared New Caledonia the crown colony of British Columbia.

Governor Douglas had another advantage over the forces of lawlessness: Judge Matthew Baillie Begbie. Appointed in 1858, Begbie toured backwoods settlements and mining camps throughout the Interior, meting out frontier justice from horseback, tent, and barroom.

Begbie's approach was clear. "I am given to understand that the mining class of the western states look upon liberty as a condition of life which gives them the right to defy the laws of their country,

Top: Among those rushing to the Cariboo goldfields was a Cornishman named Billy Barker who jumped ship in Victoria in 1858. He arrived early in 1862 at Williams Creek where he struck it rich later that year. The town that sprang up around his claim became known as Barkerville.

Bottom: Soon after Billy Barker's strike, Barkerville was calling itself the largest town west of Chicago and north of San Francisco. A fire destroyed the town in 1868, and although it was quickly rebuilt, Barkerville never fully recovered.

and to govern it according to their wishes by the might of Bowie knife and Colt's revolver," he was to tell one accused man. "We have a law which prohibits the use of [such] weapons, and ... I will punish most severely all those who, coming into this British colony, make use of such deadly weapons."

Although he became known as "the hanging judge" for his tough, no-nonsense approach to the law, Begbie was regarded as effective and fair, contributing greatly to the early development of the province.

Gold is elusive. Unlike dreams, which can keep renewing themselves, the seductive metal eventually plays out. By late 1859, rich gold finds on the lower Fraser were becoming scarce. Some of the miners headed farther north to the Cariboo. In the winter of 1860, "Dutch" William Dietz found rich deposits of gold in the gravel of Williams Creek, leading to the establishment of Barkerville, perhaps the most famous of the gold rush settlements.

The town was named after Billy Barker, one of many miners of the era who made a fortune overnight, but died penniless. In 1862, Barker had dug a shaft 13 metres deep and was just about to give

Top: Barkerville's Chinatown. By 1862, between 2500 and 4000 Chinese lived in BC. Many came from poor and overcrowded conditions in south China looking for *gim shan,* "the gold mountain." Diligent workers, they were often resented and tended to live together in Chinatowns throughout the Interior.

Bottom: Cameron Claim 1865. One of the richest claims in the Cariboo belonged to John "Cariboo" Cameron, yielding from 40 to 112 ounces of gold, three shifts a day. Although Cameron eventually took $350,000 out of his claim, the personal cost was great. His daughter died while the family was en route to the goldfields in 1862 and his wife died a year later, before Cameron found gold.

Above: Among the engineering marvels along the Cariboo Wagon Road is the Alexandra Suspension Bridge, built in 1861 by Joseph Trutch. Although Trutch had never attempted a project of this size, his design, which included two four-inch cables of woven wire, was capable of supporting a three-ton load. The bridge still stands near Spuzzum today.

Left: In 1862 Governor James Douglas let contracts for the construction of the Cariboo Wagon Road, which was completed to Barkerville in 1865. The road had to be blasted out of solid rock in places and supported by log cribbing in others. It was destroyed during CPR construction in the 1880s.

Top: "Bull-punchers" drove ox teams, such as these at Boston Bar in 1882, by walking beside them with a stick or whip. Oxen could out-pull horses but were slower, averaging only three to six kilometres a day. The bull-punchers claimed they could carry cargo as varied as eggs and mining machinery on the same load without breakage. An average team consisted of 10 animals, each ox capable of pulling a tonne of freight.

Bottom: Francis Barnard, an enterprising 30-year-old, arrived in Yale in 1859 with $5 in his pocket. By 1865 travellers could take his Barnard's Express, popularly known as the BX Line, from Yale to Barkerville.

up when he hit pay dirt. He and his partners dug $600,000 in gold from the claim, triggering a rush that saw the town's population swell to estimates as high as 20,000. Hotels, banks, barbershops, and restaurants made Barkerville the centre of mining life. The town also had a newspaper, a theatre, touring companies, a library, a resident poet, an amateur theatrical society, several churches, a Chinatown, and the famous Hurdy Gurdy girls, who would cavort with the miners for $10 a dance.

With the discovery of the Cariboo goldfields, Douglas had another problem on his hands:

transportation of goods and supplies. Yale was the terminus of the paddlewheeler route from the coast. North of Yale, the raging waters of the Fraser Canyon made the river impassable all the way to Soda Creek, some 400 kilometres upstream. Access to the Cariboo was limited to the two fur brigade trails from Hope and Yale to Kamloops, and a precarious Native path along the Fraser Canyon.

Envisioning starvation, price gouging, rioting, and the loss of valuable revenue, Douglas contracted for construction of the Cariboo Wagon Road. Completed in 1865, it was the major

Above: One of the more imaginative schemes to make money during the Cariboo Gold Rush was the "Dromedary Express." Since camels could carry heavy loads and go for days without food or water, the idea seemed feasible. The men hoped to make $60,000 the first season, but the animals' ill temper, foul smell, and tender feet made short work of their plan. The camels were released into the desert near Cache Creek in 1864. G. Smith (left) and A. MacPhail posed with the last camel, which died in the Okanagan ca. 1905.

STEAM TO CARIBOO !

The British Columbia
:ENERAL TRANSPORTATION COMPANY

Vill place Four of THOMSON'S PATENT ROAD STEAM
:RS on the route between Yale and Barkerville in the Firs
Veek in April, and will be prepared to enter into Contracts fo
le conveyance of Freight from Yale to Soda Creek in Eigh
|AYS. Through Contracts will be made as soon as the conditioi

Above: A project of Francis Barnard, this early attempt to haul freight over the Cariboo Road by mechanical means was also doomed to failure. The rubber-tired road steamers were imported from Scotland in 1871, but couldn't conquer the steep grade of Jackass Mountain in the Fraser Canyon. The engine was later used to help log near present-day Jericho in Vancouver.

route north until the Canadian Pacific Railway came through 20 years later.

Entrepreneurs built roadhouses that offered food and lodging to weary travellers. Towns and communities such as 100 Mile House, named for their distance along the route from Lillooet, began as stopovers on the stage-coach route. While some had good reputations, others were less appealing. Early traveller Matthew Macfie compared the hostelry at 70 Mile House with a robber's cave. "The floor [is] covered with blanketed bodies," he wrote. "On the counter sleeps the barkeeper, to guard the liquors from any traveller that might, in a fit of thirst, so far forget himself as to get up in the night, put forth his hand without permission, and moisten his throat."

Not all prospectors looking for the Cariboo goldfields used the Cariboo Wagon Road. In the spring

Above: In 1868, Soda Creek served as the transfer point between paddlewheeler and stage coach on the Cariboo Wagon Road. The bearded man leaning against the post in front of the doorway on the left is Peter Dunlevy, one of the miners who discovered gold in 1859 on the Horsefly River, one of the earliest claims in the Cariboo Gold Rush.

Left: While most gold seekers travelled to the Cariboo goldfields up the Fraser River from New Westminster, a group of "Overlanders" attempted the trip via the Rocky Mountains. Catherine Schubert was the only woman on the trip. Two days after completing the treacherous journey down the North Thompson River, she gave birth to a baby girl at Kamloops.

Top: Although the gold discoveries at Wild Horse Creek weren't as long-lived as those in the Cariboo, 5000 prospectors were attracted to the area in 1864, when claims paid from $300 to $1000 per day. Goldpanners like Jim White, Charlie Smith, Pete Lum, and Theirsa Johnson continued to try their luck in the early 1900s.

Bottom: Fort Steele 1898. Fort Steele began as Galbraith's Ferry during the Wild Horse Gold Rush. Irishman John Galbraith started a ferry service across the Kootenay and St. Mary's rivers when he arrived in 1865. The town faded in the 1870s, regained momentum in the 1890s, but suffered a severe setback in 1898 when the CPR put its Crowsnest line through Cranbrook.

of 1862, attracted by the British Columbia Overland Transit Company's promise of "the speediest, safest and most economical route to the [Cariboo] gold diggings," a group of 250 set out from St. Paul, Minnesota to cross the Rocky Mountains.

After a gruelling journey over the Prairies in bumpy Red River carts, some gave up the dream at Fort Edmonton in August. Those remaining divided into two groups at Tête Jaune Cache. One group would travel down the North Thompson River to Kamloops, the other would follow the Fraser.

Both journeys were perilous. The story of a man named Chapman is particularly chilling. Before attempting the difficult rapids of the Fraser's Grand Canyon, Chapman wrote in his journal, then left it and his jacket on shore. Once in the rapids, Chapman's raft got caught in a whirlpool and he went under. On shore, his colleagues retrieved his belongings and read his last journal entry: "Arrived at Grand Canyon, ran the rapids, and was drowned."

The effect of the gold rush on settlement was not limited to the Fraser River drainage. Drovers Cornelius O'Keefe and Thomas Greenhow, on their way to the Cariboo with a herd of cattle for the miners, were attracted by the natural grazing land and mild climate in the Okanagan Valley when they passed through in 1866. They returned a year

Above left: In 1863, while thousands of men and women were heading to the Cariboo goldfields in the hopes of striking it rich, Viscount Milton (right) and Dr. Walter Cheadle (centre) arrived as the area's first tourists. Cheadle's *Northwest Passage by Land,* telling of their journey across Canada, enjoyed nine printings between 1865 and 1891. The men are pictured here in San Francisco in 1863, with Cariboo politician George Walkem.

Above right: One of the heroes of the Interior's early development was Edgar Dewdney, who built the Dewdney Trail across the southern part of the province in the 1860s. He had a long career of public service, including a term as lieutenant-governor of BC (1892–1897).

Opposite: The Kutenai people were indigenous to the Wild Horse area. In 1887 Superintendent Sam Steele of the North West Mounted Police was called in to settle a dispute between the remaining Wild Horse settlers and the Kutenai. Among Steele's conciliatory actions was compensation for Native land that had been taken away at Cranbrook.

later, and O'Keefe created a huge cattle ranch near present-day Vernon that was operational until the 1960s.

It was also during this time that Father Charles Pandosy of the Oblate Order of Mary the Immaculate established the first permanent settlement in the Okanagan. In 1860, the group built Okanagan Mission just south of present-day Kelowna.

Raised in France, Pandosy arrived in North America in 1847, spending several years with Native people in Washington Territory before political events forced him north. American authorities suspected him of inappropriate sympathy for the Natives. When asked for advice by a Native chief,

Pandosy had replied: "The whites will take your country as they have taken other countries from the Indians. I came from the land of the white man, far to the east, where the people are thicker than the grass on the hills. Where there are only a few here now, others will come with each year until your country will be overrun with them. I cannot advise you or help you. I wish I could."

The fathers also established a post office and planted the first fruit trees and vineyards in the Okanagan Valley – an area now famous for its wineries and orchard industry.

Prospectors were making other gold discoveries east of Hope in the Similkameen, Kettle, and Columbia river systems.

Two American soldiers accidentally discovered gold at Rock Creek in 1859, triggering a brief but frantic rush there.

As in the fur-trading days, the north-south valleys of the southern Interior gave Douglas cause for concern. American prospectors could travel north to British Columbian goldfields and south again without paying taxes or mining fees. American businesses would happily sell the miners whatever supplies they needed, another loss of revenue for the struggling colony.

At the same time Douglas was contracting for the Cariboo Road, he hired Englishman Edgar Dewdney to build a trail between Hope and Princeton. In 1861

Dewdney and civil engineer Walter Moberly (who in the 1870s contracted as a surveyor for the transcontinental railway) finished the trail as far as Rock Creek.

In 1863 gold was discovered at Wild Horse Creek in the East Kootenay and, by the following June, hundreds of miners headed to this new El Dorado. Dewdney extended the trail farther east. Discovery of gold at the Big Bend of the Columbia River lured miners from the towns built up around the Wild Horse strike in 1865, and the road fell into disrepair. Concentrated settlement of the Kootenays would have to wait another 20 years.

By the late 1860s, the nature of gold mining was changing in the Cariboo and southern Interior. The

Top: A contingent of 75 North West Mounted Police accompanied Steele, setting up camp on the heights above the ferry. Grateful for Steele's peaceful handling of the problem, residents renamed their settlement Fort Steele in 1888.

Bottom: Osoyoos Court House, 1874. Cattle ranchers settled the Okanagan in the 1860s. This customs house at Osoyoos was built in 1861. Third from the left is Judge Haynes, gold commissioner and customs officer in the 1860s and 1870s. His son Val, seated third from right, was the first European child born in the Okanagan.

Top: Drovers herded cattle to Barkerville from south of the border and found the land on the way highly appealing. Cornelius O'Keefe was on his way to the Cariboo with a herd of cattle when he decided the lush grazing land of the Okanagan would be a good place to settle. Thadeus and Jerome Harper acquired the massive Gang Ranch during the 1870s after ranching in the Kamloops area in the 1860s.

Bottom: Rancher Thomas Ellis arrived in the Okanagan in 1865. His homestead, pictured here in the 1860s, is the site of present-day Penticton. By 1885 Ellis was the largest landholder in the Okanagan with 3750 head of cattle and 12,000 hectares. He drove his cattle over 400 kilometres to Hope.

days were over when nuggets could be picked out of pockets of gravel. In places like Barkerville, the gold was deep beneath the ground. Machines were needed. Syndicates were formed. Individual miners headed farther north or left the colony. The boom years were ending.

Governor James Douglas, who had managed the potentially unruly gold rush years with a strong hand, retired in 1864. In 1866, the two colonies of Vancouver Island and British Columbia united. But with the economy faltering, the new colony of British Columbia faced an uncertain future.

The National Dream

As the dream of gold faded, a new vision emerged in the colony of British Columbia: Confederation with the British North American colonies of Canada, New Brunswick, and Nova Scotia.

BC supporters of the union saw it as a solution to the colony's economic problems. They thought a transcontinental wagon road and increased trade with the East held obvious benefits. But the idea was not universally embraced in BC. Limited settlement on the Prairie provinces, a distrust of eastern politicians, allegiance to Britain, and the desire of some to unite with the US, were among the reasons for popular opposition. In 1867, when the Dominion of Canada was formed, BC was not among the signatories.

But in January 1871, after strenuous lobbying by men like Amor De Cosmos and political maneuvering that saw pro-Confederationist Anthony Musgrave become governor of the colony, BC joined the Dominion of Canada. "Clad in bridal attire, she is about to unite her destinies with a country which is prepared to do much for her," blushed the *British Colonist* on New Year's Day in 1871.

The anticipation was justified. The terms of Confederation promised not just a road, but a national railway to connect BC with the eastern provinces. Construction was to begin within two years and be completed in ten. The agreement would bring dramatic changes to BC's Interior.

Amalgamation with Canada came none too soon. Five years before, Barkerville had been a town of ten to twenty thousand, but in 1871 the entire non-Native population of the Cariboo dropped to 2000. Only 1000 people lived in Hope, Yale, and Boston Bar, with another three or four hundred in Lillooet, Mile 0 on the Cariboo Wagon Road. Scattered pockets of Hudson's Bay men, missionaries, a few miners in the Omineca gold fields and the Kootenays, and some settlers on the isolated ranches of the Okanagan and Similkameen barely populated the region.

However, the joyful Canadian Confederation marriage soon became rocky. When the time came to ratify the terms of Confederation, many eastern politicians balked at building an expensive railroad across the country to such a sparsely populated area. Although the federal government

Opposite: Known as "Slaughter Run" to laborers, this portion of the CPR route typifies the difficulties facing surveyors and construction workers during the 1870s and 1880s. This 1881 photograph shows Tunnel Number 7 under construction 38 kilometres north of Yale on the Fraser Canyon. Part of the boon to the local economy included establishing dynamite factories necessary for blasting the solid bedrock. The construction of the rail line obliterated portions of the 20-year-old Cariboo Wagon Road.

awarded the construction contract to Sir Hugh Allan and quickly sent surveyors to BC, by 1873 work had not yet started.

That same year, the Pacific Scandal broke when Prime Minister Macdonald wired Allan, "I must have another ten thousand." Newspapers revealed that Macdonald and his colleagues had accepted over $360,000 in illicit campaign funds in return for railway contracts. The government that had promised the railway was defeated.

Animosity grew between the federal and provincial representatives. Lord Dufferin, Governor General of Canada, travelled west on a diplomatic mission in 1876, but the situation didn't improve. In 1878, politician Amor De Cosmos made a dramatic motion in BC's provincial assembly to secede from Confederation. Many feel De Cosmos' motion was nothing more than a political gesture, but we will never know. Macdonald's reelection that same year brought a recommitment to a national railway.

The Canadian Pacific Railway company, with Donald A. Smith, J.J. Hill, and George Stephen at the helm, incorporated on February 15, 1881. In return for the difficult construction task ahead, the company received generous and controversial terms including 25 million dollars in cash, 10 million hectares of land, 37 million dollars for surveys, and a 20-year

Above: Surveyors at Fort McLeod, 1879. George Mercer Dawson (standing in centre) may have been short in stature but his "superior mental and observational powers" gave the geologist a towering reputation. His surveys of BC during the 1870s strongly influenced subsequent decisions regarding the route of the CPR. Some suggest Dawson and his colleagues put the "Fort Misery" sign over the door as a comment on the swarms of mosquitoes that plagued their work, evidenced by the netting tucked on top of their hat brims.

transportation monopoly for routes south to the US. William Cornelius Van Horne, appointed general manager of the railway, oversaw the monumental construction task.

Although early surveyors had considered the ideal route through the Rocky Mountains to be via the Yellowhead Pass west of Jasper, others favored a more southerly route through the central Rockies. The Kicking Horse Pass had been surveyed through the central Rocky Mountains by the Palliser Expedition in 1858, and Walter Moberly had discovered the Eagle Pass through the Monashee Mountains to the west in 1865. But astoundingly, when the first workers began building track in Yale in 1880, surveyors still hadn't found the route through the mountains to connect the Kicking Horse and Eagle passes.

Luckily, railway builders are an obstinate lot. In 1882, Major A.B. "Hell's Bells" Rogers, no doubt somewhat inspired by the promise of a $5000 bonus and his name on the map, found a pass through the Selkirk Mountains. Described as tough as the landscape he faced in his work, Rogers was a Yale graduate who sported an outrageous moustache,

swore unreservedly, and liked chewing-tobacco and raw beans. Although his underlings found him irascible and cantankerous, he possessed remarkable determination. Today the Rogers Pass is one of the most famous attractions on the Trans-Canada Highway.

Tenacity was probably part of the job description of all early railway builders. In 1879, Andrew Onderdonk, a 30-year-old engineer from New York, obtained the contracts to build the railway from Port Moody to Kamloops and

Above: The son of a wealthy New York family, 30-year-old Andrew Onderdonk had just finished building the seawall in San Francisco when he purchased four Fraser Canyon CPR construction contracts for $215,000 in 1879. His crews began work at Yale in May 1880.

through the Eagle Pass to the east over some of the most difficult terrain on the CPR line.

Work on the line progressed slowly through the rugged terrain of the Fraser Canyon and Onderdonk met many difficulties. Unable to find enough skilled workers, he imported thousands of Chinese laborers. When freight costs were too high, Onderdonk built his own boat and succeeded at sending it through the notorious Hell's Gate Canyon – a task previously declared impossible.

Completion of the CPR took four and a half years and 30,000 workers. Donald Smith drove the last spike at Craigellachie just west of Revelstoke on November 7, 1885. The first passenger train arrived in Port Moody on July 4, 1886.

The CPR provided a transportation route for resources to go out of the province, stimulating the economy through logging, mining, and agriculture. But William Cornelius Van Horne, "the ablest railway general in the world," also saw an opportunity to make the line pay for itself by encouraging tourism.

To avoid hauling a dining car up the steep grades near Field in the Rocky Mountains, the company built Mt. Stephen House in 1886. With spectacular scenery so near at hand, it soon became a popular destination for tourists, artists, and climbers. Glacier House, built in 1887 beneath the magnificent Illecillewaet

Above: Onderdonk received a 13-gun salute when he arrived in Yale in April 1880. The townspeople had much to celebrate. Although Yale was still the head of navigation for the lower Fraser River, gold rush prosperity had faded. The railway would bring needed jobs to the region.

Top: Financing was a constant problem for the CPR. Among the engineering challenges that raised the cost was this cantilevered bridge over the Fraser River near Lytton, rightly described at the time as "one of the great wonders of the CP Railway" by Yale's *Inland Sentinel*. A mile (1.6 kilometres) of track cost about $185,000 through this rugged terrain. Onderdonk's crews built 27 tunnels and 600 trestles and bridges.

Bottom: Onderdonk had a ship specially built that would carry freight up the Fraser River through the treacherous Fraser Canyon. In 1882, 150 Chinese winched the S.S. *Skuzzy* through Hell's Gate from shore. It was the vessel's only trip on that part of the river.

Above: Chinese camp, Kamloops, 1886. Unable to find enough workers to fill his labor needs, in 1881 Onderdonk contracted with a Chinese broker to import 1500 experienced Chinese railway workers from the US and another 2000 from China and Hong Kong. Estimates vary, but by 1884 between 9000 and 17,000 Chinese lived in the province, most working on the CPR. Onderdonk estimated that three Chinese workers died for every kilometre of track that was laid.

Opposite top: The construction of the CPR stimulated the economy and settlement of the Interior in a variety of ways. Lumber was required for railway ties, snowsheds, bunkhouses, and other frame buildings. Prior to the railway, oxen (such as these pictured in 1885), pulled logs over skid roads, so named because they were made of skid logs secured in the mud.

Opposite bottom: Once the railways were built, logs could be transported more easily by flatcar. The railway provided access to huge tracts of Interior forests and a method of transporting lumber to the Prairies, although the Interior logging industry didn't become viable until the mid-20th century.

Glacier near Rogers Pass, was also a major attraction. In Golden, the CPR went so far as to build replica chalets for the Swiss guides it hired to accompany tourists on treks through the Rocky and Columbia mountains.

Despite the obvious benefits that tourism promotion gave to the CPR's balance sheets, Van Horne is well remembered for his advocacy of national parks. He successfully lobbied for Banff, Yoho, and Glacier national parks, which were established in 1885 and 1886.

During the next decade, the CPR developed an even more intensive plan to exploit the natural beauty of the Interior. The company planned and built

Above: "The Last Spike," driven at Craigellachie on November 7, 1885, is perhaps Canada's most famous photograph. Donald A. Smith wields the mallet, with CPR General Manager William Cornelius Van Horne slightly to Smith's right. Behind Smith in the tall hat, stands Sir Sandford Fleming, who had supported a more northerly route through the Yellowhead Pass.

Opposite: Kamloops began during the fur-trade years and flourished again in the gold-rush era. In the 1870s, the railroad brought new life to the town as a headquarters for railway construction.

elegant hotels on Okanagan, Arrow, and Kootenay lakes and operated luxuriously appointed paddlewheelers. The service attracted visitors, provided a regular and frequent schedule that enhanced the new agricultural industries, and stimulated land settlement.

While Confederation solved some of the Interior's post-gold rush problems, it created a different set of problems for the Native population.

As settlers began creating towns and fencing ranchland, many Native tribes, barred from land to which they previously had free access, were assigned reserve lands. In British Columbia, unlike other areas of Canada, there were few treaties. The federal government divided BC into 20 districts governed by Indian agents responsible for the welfare of the Natives.

Although Roman Catholic, Anglican, and Methodist missionaries had been operating in the Interior since the fur-trading days, the federal government now gave the missionaries subsidies to

Above: Revelstoke owes its existence to the CPR. Just a few kilometres east of Craigellachie, the town is pictured here in 1889. Called Big Eddy, Second Crossing, and then Farwell, the town got the name it retains today in 1886, when English banker Lord Revelstoke invested in the CPR.

Opposite: Among the inspection devices used on the early line was a hand-pumped car, pictured here in 1885. Contractors could inspect the tracks in only slightly more comfort in a steam-operated device.

Top: Washouts, slides, and avalanches created constant problems for efficient operation of the railroad. This weird and wonderful machine, "a washout structure," was photographed in 1903.

Bottom: "His occupation gone." This photograph, from Andrew Onderdonk's collection, allegedly shows the first Native man hired by the CPR at the completion of railway construction. Not only was the man now out of work, but in the three decades since the first onslaught of Europeans into BC's Interior, his way of life had undergone unimaginable changes.

Opposite: Once CPR construction was complete, the mountainous terrain of the Interior continued to plague the smooth operation of the railway. In 1910, a disastrous slide in the Rogers Pass buried a crew of 62 men. Only one man survived. In 1916, the construction of the Connaught Tunnel eliminated the route over the pass.

Above: Confederation gave the federal government responsibility for Native people. Christian missionaries, notably Roman Catholics and Anglicans wishing to convert the Natives, established schools and missions throughout the Interior. St. Joseph's Mission in Williams Lake, pictured above, was one of several Roman Catholic facilities in the Interior.

Opposite: Often Native children were separated from their parents, forced to wear Western clothes, and forbidden to speak their own languages. These children are learning knitting and sewing from the Sisters of the Child Jesus, St. Joseph's Mission, ca. 1900.

Right: To pay for the railway, William Cornelius Van Horne, who became president of the CPR in 1888 and chairman of the board in 1899, began promoting the railway to tourists. Possible destinations were quickly expanded as the corporation acquired shipping lines and eventually airlines.

Glacier Hotel, C.
Photo by R. Maynard, Victoria

Opposite: Rather than haul a dining car up the steep grades of the Selkirk Range, in 1886 the CPR built Glacier House at the foot of Illecillewaet Glacier. Glacier House and Mt. Stephen House at Field became popular destinations for artists, hikers, and tourists.

Top right: Illecillewaet, also known as the "Great Glacier," has since receded, but in 1886 its icy edge was just a short hike from the railway line. The development of mountaineering in North America resulted in large part from the construction of the CPR and the company's subsequent promotion of the Rocky Mountains.

Middle right: Mt. Stephen House in Field was also built to avoid hauling the heavy dining cars up the steep grades.

Bottom right: The interior of the Mt. Stephen House dining room, shown here in 1887, typifies the elegant CPR style.

operate residential and day schools. Here, removed from their families and communities, Native children were forced to speak English and adopt European customs and values.

Enforced acculturation took its toll. By 1900, the Native population in BC dropped to about 25,000, one-quarter of its size a century earlier.

Above: Attractions for early tourists included the Continental Divide. Rivers and streams flowing east of here empty into the Arctic Ocean or Hudson Bay. Those flowing west empty into the Pacific Ocean.

Opposite top: Mountain climbers in the 19th century were reluctant to venture forth without a guide. In 1899, the CPR hired two Swiss guides, Edward Feuz, Sr. and Christian Häsler, Sr., to lead excursions from Mt. Stephen and Glacier houses. Within two years, eight men provided guiding services.

Opposite bottom: Ascending Illecillewaet Glacier, ca. 1910. Over the next 50 years, the Swiss, including Feuz's three sons, continued to guide climbers. Ed Feuz Jr. recalled, "We had to chop a few steps going up with the ice axe and rope the people on and go up with them."

Ascending the Illecillewaet Glacier, B. C.

Silver, Lead, and Hell

Although the CPR brought a rush of prosperity to the Interior during the early 1880s, when the railway was completed many who had depended on its construction for their livelihood were left without means of support.

Among them were Osner and Winslow Hall, American settlers in Washington Territory who had been supplying construction crews with food. In 1886, the Halls and

several companions, faced with crop failures and no markets, headed north along the Pend Oreille River into British Columbia to try their luck searching for placer gold. It is a recurrent theme in gold rush tales, but the party was just about to give up and return home when they hit pay dirt on Toad Mountain near present-day Nelson.

They may have dreamed of gold, but the Hall party discovered silver, and prospectors flocked to the area, re-creating the frenzied days of the Cariboo Gold Rush. A chain reaction of discoveries occurred in the East and West Kootenays and the Boundary region. While "silver, lead, and hell," were raised in the Silvery Slocan, the boom also raised communities. In 1886 for example, not a single

Above: Launched in 1892, the S.S. *Ainsworth* was one of several sternwheelers transporting ore and passengers between Kootenay Lake and Bonner's Ferry, Idaho. Sternwheelers played an important part in early transportation in the province, requiring only a "hint of dew" for sailing. One story tells of a passenger on a Thompson River vessel who fell overboard and raised a cloud of dust. It was said only teetotallers travelled on the tiny *Ainsworth* because it was so cramped there was no room to bend an elbow. The vessel sunk in a storm on the lake in November 1898.

Above: Hall Mines Smelter, 1897. The Hall Brothers from Colville, Washington led a party that discovered a rich ore deposit on Toad Mountain, starting the mining boom in the Kootenays. The Halls sold their Silver King Mine for 1.8 million dollars in 1893 without ever starting serious production. The smelter was built in 1895.

Opposite: Developers built this tramway in 1896 to transport ore from Silver King Mine's 1500-metre elevation to the city of Nelson below. It was the largest system of its kind in the world, operating entirely by gravity, with the empty buckets pulled uphill as the full ones went down. The mine continued production until 1915.

town stood in the West Kootenay. By 1901, almost 25,000 permanent residents lived there. But for many survival was a struggle.

Although no written confirmation exists, some say that eminent Scottish botanist David Douglas (for whom Douglas fir is named) first discovered the rich ore deposits on Kootenay Lake when he explored the area in the 1820s. However, the earliest attempt to file a claim on the lake was made by Henry Doan in the early 1870s.

Doan took samples of rich silver-lead ore from a site north of present-day Kootenay Bay to San Francisco and caught the attention of several investors. When mining expert George Hearst arrived to test on-site samples, Doan confessed to "salting" the ore to make it seem richer than it was. (Doan disappeared into Washington, but Hearst later made a fortune in mining, became a US senator, and sired William Randolph Hearst, the American newspaper tycoon.)

Above: Interior of the Hall Mines Smelter. The smelter was possibly the largest in the world in 1897, when this photograph was taken. Its crucible was capable of producing 250 tonnes of ore per day. The ore contained silver and copper, with some gold.

Top: As news of the Kootenay mining boom spread, hotels were quickly slapped together to accommodate the influx of people. "Some set up good grub and some don't. Some have beds with spring mattresses and some have beds without mattresses," one patron wrote in 1889. Nelson's Royal Hotel, serving customers in 1898 in this photograph, still operates today.

Bottom: Progressive Nelson had its own power plant and streetcar system. The hilly town boasted not only the smallest system in the British Empire, but at 11 percent, its line also climbed one of the steepest grades. These schoolchildren are likely celebrating Empire Day during the Boer War, ca. 1902. Despite its proximity to the US and the preponderance of American miners, many Nelson residents maintained strong ties with Britain.

197. NELSON, B.C., HORSE RACE, JULY 1st, 1898.

Despite a discouraging report from Hearst, prospectors continued to examine the area. For a while, it seemed bad luck was the only result. In 1882, Robert Sproule, a fugitive from Washington, staked a claim on Doan's site. However, Sproule became involved in an ownership dispute with Thomas Hammill, and the court decided in favor of Hammill, who had the backing of wealthy mining interests. In 1885 Hammill was murdered while working his claim and Sproule was hanged for the crime the following year.

Eastern mining interests developed the mine in 1887, and the luck associated with the mineral deposit changed – the Bluebell became one of the longest-operating mines in the West Kootenay region. Within three years workers had extracted over 1.5 million tonnes of ore and driven 465 metres of workings beneath the earth's surface. In 1895, a smelter was built at Pilot Bay, just south of the Bluebell. And the town of Riondel grew up near the mine itself.

Although prospectors still dreamed and panned for gold on gravel bars, the riches of the Kootenay mountains lay deep underground and their development depended on capital

Above: What started as a tent city of 400 in 1887 became a town of 7000 a decade later. Originally known as Stanley, the settlement was renamed Salisbury and then incorporated as Nelson in 1897. Nelson residents celebrated Dominion Day in 1898 with a horse race down the main street.

Top: A world depression in the 1890s attracted many to the Kootenay-Boundary region as word spread of its mining activity. In 1897, early photographer Mattie Gunterman and her family trekked from Seattle to the prosperous Lardeau region, travelling part of the way over the old Dewdney Trail.

Bottom: The Lardeau area at the north end of Kootenay Lake prospered greatly during the 1890s. Trout Lake City, Poplar Creek, and Ferguson – now ghost towns – supported vital and lively communities. In this 1900 photograph, visitors rest outside Emma Jowett's cabin at the Foggy Day Mine. Jowett operated the Windsor Hotel in Trout Lake City until the 1950s. The hotel was still operating in 1990.

Above: Mattie Gunterman titled this 1900 photograph "The Aristocracy of Ferguson." Ferguson was the centre of Lardeau mining activity, boasting its own newspaper, five hotels, an opera house, saloons, electricity, waterworks, a population of 1000, and a rosy future. Oldtimers say the profits from area mines built the parliament buildings in Victoria.

from big business. From 1905 to 1921, the Bluebell Mine was operated by the Canadian Metal Company with head offices in Paris, France.

Farther down the lake, the Hall brothers' incredibly rich Silver King Mine led to the establishment of the city of Nelson. British backers took over the mine's operation in 1893, a smelter was built in 1895, and the town was incorporated in 1897.

In 1890, Joe Moris and Joe Bourgeois, two more prospectors from Washington, staked several claims on Red Mountain farther west. Fate had a hand in this development as well. Miners were limited in the number of claims they could make, so they offered another prospector,

E.S.Topping, the extension to their Centre Star Mine – if he could come up with the $12.50 fee to cover all the claims. Topping did, and his Le Roi Mine turned out to be one of the most lucrative gold mines in the province. Four years later, Ross Thompson laid out the town of Rossland at the foot of Red Mountain, and another rollicking mining town was born.

Beginning in 1891, prospectors made important discoveries in the Slocan area as well. Sandon, Ainsworth, Kaslo, New Denver, and Silverton are among the towns that flourished with the discovery of rich ore deposits. The editor of the Slocan newspaper, Robert Tecumseh Lowery, wrote, "Silver, lead, and hell are

Above: The ore-laden mountains provided enormous transportation challenges. In 1906, the Crawford Tram Company of Nelson used 31 pack horses to haul 1100 metres of five-centimetre cable to the Silver Dollar Mine above Camborne in the Lardeau area. The mine was likely building a system similar to Nelson's Silver King Mine to transport ore down the mountain.

Left: Many stood more chance of winning at poker than of striking it rich in the Lardeau. Developers often took advantage of inexperienced miners. "Fictitious boosting," as described in a BC government mining report, "made it both difficult to raise money for legitimate propositions and for the prospectors to get either grubstakes or encouragement." Hopefully, these card players photographed by Gunterman in 1899 at the Prospector's Exchange Saloon in Beaton, had more luck.

Above: Many early communities had to struggle against disasters to survive. In February 1894, a fire destroyed much of the business district in Kaslo. The district had seen record snowfalls the previous winter, and when extremely hot May temperatures melted the snowpack quickly, severe flooding resulted. Gale-force winds and torrential rainstorms made the situation worse in June. At the height of the flooding, paddlewheelers landed in the centre of Kaslo. The disaster destroyed over 70 homes and businesses, but townspeople quickly rebuilt.

Right: Kaslo fought with other area towns for supremacy during the boom years. As the terminus for the Kaslo and Slocan (K&S) Railway, the town became an important service centre. Despite the disasters of 1894, hundreds of spectators watched this baseball game that same year.

Opposite: The 2900-metre sheer dropoff at Payne Bluff symbolized the tenuous position of the K&S Railway. Only 54 kilometres long, the narrow-gauge line was part of the ongoing war for rail domination between the (American) Great Northern and the Canadian Pacific railways. Operated by GNR, the K&S first transported ore from Sandon to Kaslo in 1895, challenging the CPR's Nakusp and Slocan line. From Kaslo, the ore was shipped to Bonner's Ferry, Idaho. When the expansion of the Trail smelter made American processing uneconomical, the GNR lost interest. In 1910, a forest fire twisted rail lines and destroyed stations and bridges, spelling the end of the K&S.

Above: In 1898, Sandon was the capital of the "Silvery Slocan" and one of the largest communities in the Interior. The terminus of two rail lines, it had over 20 hotels, an opera house, and a population estimated as high as 10,000. The Slocan was one of the richest silver areas in North America.

raised in the Slocan, and unless you can take a hand in producing these articles your services are not required."

Sandon is one of the most famous of the towns that flourished during this time. Supported by two railways, Sandon had 24 hotels, 23 saloons, an opera house, and its own hydro-electric plant. Now, along with dozens of towns that once shared promising futures, Sandon is a ghost town, the dreams of its inhabitants buried in the past.

Farther east, miners were making discoveries in the Purcell Mountains not far from Wild Horse Creek, the site of the 1860s gold rush in the East Kootenay. In 1892, E.C. Smith, John Cleaver, Pat

Sullivan, and Walter Burchett founded the great Sullivan Mine at present-day Kimberley, which would become the largest lead-zinc-silver mine in the world. They had been attracted to the area by Joe Bourgeois' discovery of valuable ore at North Star Mountain earlier that year.

In 1895, the 24-year-old "boy wonder" of American mining, F. Augustus Heinze, erected a small smelter at Trail Creek Landing on the Columbia River to process the ore from Red Mountain. In 1898, Heinze sold his interests to the Canadian Pacific Railway. The construction of the smelter had an impact on several settlements in the Kootenays. Plans for smelters in Nakusp on the

Above: Built between 1892 and 1895, this stretch of the K&S Railway shows the extensive cribbing needed for lines in the mountainous area, where avalanches and slides were a constant problem. The need for cribbing, railway ties, and lumber for buildings was one of many economic side-benefits of the mining boom.

Left: These miners are engaged in a rock-drilling contest in Sandon in 1904. The man kneeling over the hole clasps the drill, giving it a quarter-turn each time his partner (back to camera) hits the drill with a sledge or mallet.

Opposite: Some of these loggers in the Lardeau area in the 1890s are standing on springboards – two-metre-long, hand-made planks. The planks were fitted at one end with a crescent-shaped iron plate that fit into a wedge cut in the tree. Made of clear-grained fir, the boards had a certain resiliency, thus "springboards." Raised above the swollen butt-ends of the tree, the men used two- to three-metre-long saws known as "gut fiddles" or "misery whips" to fell the tree.

Arrow Lakes and Marysville near Kimberley dissolved, and the Pilot Bay smelter on Kootenay Lake closed in favor of the Trail development. The CPR's Consolidated Mining and Smelting Company operation (Cominco) became one of the largest lead-zinc smelters in the world.

The development of Kootenay and Boundary area mines had a double benefit to settlement. Not only did the new kind of mining foster stable communities such as Grand Forks, Nelson, and Kimberley, but it also encouraged railways – dozens of them. Their construction opened up transportation routes and encouraged more settlement.

Since the landforms in the southern Interior favor north-south rather than east-west traffic, financial backing and many of the miners themselves came from the United States. There was a much closer alliance with American cities like Spokane, Washington and Butte, Montana than BC's coastal centres of New Westminster and Victoria. American-based transportation companies such as J.J. Hill's Great Northern Railway were only too happy to transport Interior ore south of the border and enjoy the fruits of the increased trade. But the practice caused business and political leaders to worry anew about American domination of the southern Interior.

Above: Workers made dimension lumber at mills such as the Yale-Columbia Company in Nakusp, shown here in 1897. Nakusp was originally destined to have a smelter, but the expansion of Trail's facility put an end to the plans. The town survived as an important stop on the Arrow Lakes paddlewheel route.

Opposite top: Trail's smelter, shown in this 1908 photograph, was built in 1895 by 24-year-old millionaire F. Augustus Heinze, originally as a small facility to process ore from Red Mountain. When word got around that the Montana mining genius was investing in the area, others took that as an endorsement of the claims being made and hurried to get in on the potential profits.

Opposite bottom: In 1898 Heinze sold his mining interests in the Trail Creek area to the CPR for one million dollars. At first the CPR was only interested in the Columbia and Western railway charter that Heinze owned, but when Heinze insisted, the company bought the smelter, too. The CPR soon expanded the smelter and Trail became a "company town." In this 1907 photograph, workers line up on payday.

Above: In 1900, Granby Consolidated Mining and Smelting constructed a copper smelter at Grand Forks that at one time was the largest in Canada. This 1918 photograph shows blister copper pouring into molds. The smelter closed the following year after processing 13 million tonnes of ore.

Opposite top: Grand Forks in 1895 was a quiet farming community. The discovery of copper in the area led to a boom and the town's incorporation in 1897. The Kootenay-Boundary region became widely recognized as a geological bonanza. Miners had found silver in the Slocan Valley 160 kilometres to the east, gold at Red Mountain 100 kilometres east, and now copper.

Opposite bottom: Hose-reel racing was a common recreational activity in many Interior towns. These men pull the hefty fire-hose contraption in Trail in 1902. The Cominco smelter looms in the background. Of 19 smelters built in the province, the Trail facility is the only one to survive.

The battle for supremacy wasn't just about corporate profits. It was bitterly personal. Canadian J.J. Hill, head of the American-based GNR, was "the barbed-wired, shaggy-headed, one-eyed old son of a bitch of Western railroading." One of the original members of the CPR board, he developed a consuming dislike of William Cornelius Van Horne, the American who ran the CPR. Hill eventually resigned from the Canadian company vowing, "I'll get even with him if I have to go to hell for it and shovel coal!"

Their rivalry had a profound effect on the development of the southern Interior. In 1889, two years after the Hall brothers' discovery in Nelson,

Hill built the Spokane Falls and Northern Railway from Spokane to Colville, Washington, just south of the border. The railway soon extended into BC, becoming the first rail line in the Kootenays.

In response, in 1891 the CPR built the Columbia & Kootenay Railway between Nelson and Robson. From Robson, ore was shipped up the Arrow Lakes to the main CPR line at Revelstoke.

Dozens of other small railways quickly followed, such as the GNR's Kaslo and Slocan Railway and the CPR's Nakusp and Slocan line. No fewer than 27 railway charters were issued in the 1890s in the Kootenays, although only 11 were eventually built. Rival steamship lines were also

Opposite: Grand Forks is also a rich agricultural area. Mr. W.H. Covert and Mrs. Waterford Reid sold apple cider at the Grand Forks Fall Fair in 1911.

Top: In 1899, Greenwood was a busy new town, serving the growing camps that were mining copper from nearby mountains. The first claims were filed in 1886. Robert Wood founded the town in 1895 when he constructed a log store. Two years later it was an incorporated city.

Bottom: By 1901, the gigantic British Columbia Copper Company had taken over several area mines and built a smelter in Greenwood to challenge the Granby Consolidated Mining and Smelting Company's Grand Forks operation.

established on the lakes as the companies vied for transportation supremacy. During this period over 100 sternwheelers plied the lakes and rivers.

In 1897, the federal government signed an agreement with the CPR to build a rail line through the Crowsnest Pass in the Rockies and then across southern BC. Eventually, the CPR acquired 300,000 hectares in the Kootenays through the acquisition of several small railways, establishing corporate supremacy in the mining and transportation industries.

Besides being a boon to the CPR and the economy, the mining activity attracted settlement to the lush valleys of the Columbia, Kootenay, Slocan, and Okanagan river systems. Mining remained a major part of the region's economy throughout the 20th century, but many newcomers had different dreams.

Above: This panoramic view taken in the early 1900s shows the Mother Lode Mountain near Greenwood.

Right: The seemingly endless prosperity of Phoenix, one of the richest of the Boundary copper towns, collapsed in 1919, the year this photograph was taken. A prosperous town in 1900, with 1000 residents and good prospects, Phoenix was operated by the Granby Consolidated Mining and Smelting Company. The ore from claims like Old Ironsides and Knob Hill was shipped to nearby Grand Forks for processing. Two railways hauled ore to the smelter 24 hours a day, seven days a week for several years. But falling copper prices and a coal strike in the East Kootenay meant the end of the town.

Opposite: In the East Kootenay, prospectors discovered rich deposits of silver, lead, and zinc in 1892 at the North Star, Sullivan, and St. Eugene claims. In this photograph, workers watch over 5000 tonnes of North Star ore awaiting shipment at Fort Steele ca. 1895.

Opposite top: In 1897, William Fernie discovered coal in the Elk Valley area of the East Kootenay, which became known as the Pennsylvania of the West. Legend says Natives told Fernie about the source of the coal, but when he reneged on a promise to marry a chief's daughter, the woman's mother put a curse on the valley. Area mines suffered several disasters over the years, including a 1908 fire that destroyed the town of Fernie. In 1897, the CPR built its Crowsnest line largely because of the profits to be made in transporting East Kootenay coal and ore. These coke ovens are in Fernie's railyard in the early 1900s.

Opposite bottom: Even though lead, silver, zinc, and coal were the rich deposits in the East Kootenay, and large companies were taking over mining, an *arrastra* at the Dardanell Mine still operated in 1897 in the Wild Horse Creek area. After this Mexican-style water wheel pulverized the ore, miners used mercury to separate the gold.

Top right: By 1905, the CPR's Crowsnest line extended through the southern Interior from the Alberta border to Midway. But the company continued to struggle for control with its archrival the GNR. Workers actually came to blows at Midway in 1905. This construction gang works near Penticton.

Middle right: The Kettle Valley Railway opened in 1916 and ran until 1964. It not only provided transportation of goods, but also helped open the southern Interior to settlement and tourism. From Penticton's Incola Hotel, passengers could board paddlewheelers to travel up Okanagan Lake.

Bottom right: The S.S. *Sicamous* was one of the elegant CPR paddlewheelers that plied southern Interior lakes during the first half of the 20th century. Built for $180,000 in 1914, the coal-powered vessel could carry 500 passengers and travel at a speed of 17 knots. The *Sicamous* is shown in this 1919 photograph at the CPR wharf in Penticton.

Heaven on Earth

The dreams of prospectors and railway builders fuelled much of the development of BC's Interior in the late 1800s. The quick profits offered by mining and transportation attracted thousands, resulting in towns, paddlewheel routes, and railways that opened up the land.

The federal government, the CPR, and land developers soon began promoting Western Canada as an ideal place to settle – to build homes, raise families, develop communities. To those British, European, American, and eastern Canadians with few prospects, the campaign offered the dream of a better life.

In the early 1900s the Dominion Steamship Line ran an ad in several British publications that cashed in on the federal government's offer of "Free Farms of 160 Acres ... to every Male Adult of 18 years and over in the great Fertile Belt of Manitoba, Canadian North-West and British Columbia." For as little as £4 steerage, immigrants could cross the Atlantic Ocean and arrive in the country of milk and honey. Entrepreneurs talked of inexhaustible soil, ample rainfall, minimal taxes, and "no rust, no insects, and no cyclones."

Although the federal campaign aimed primarily to attract farmers to the Prairies, many newcomers continued west to British Columbia. "Grow apples, grow rich," urged promoters extolling the Kootenays. "Heaven on earth with summer weather forever," claimed an Okanagan developer.

The immigration campaign focused on northern European countries – white Anglo-Saxon Protestants were seen as the most desirable candidates. The greatest numbers of immigrants came from Britain, where jobs and prospects were scarce, and the United States, where the best land had been settled in the 19th century. In 1901, almost 12,000 British and 18,000 American immigrants arrived in Canada. By 1913, those numbers had climbed to 150,000 and 139,000 respectively. But there were also Russians (6200 in 1905), Italians (16,000 in 1901), Austrians, French, Swedish, and many other nationalities.

Absent from these statistics are large numbers of Asian immigrants. During the gold rush and railroad eras, public opinion had turned against Chinese workers. Many

Opposite: "A man could go anywhere on unoccupied Crown lands, put in a corner post, compose a rough description of one square mile of forest measured from that post, and thus secure from the Government exclusive right to the timber on that square mile," novelist Allerdale Grainger wrote in 1908. The two fallers are cutting a large Douglas fir.

Williams Lake B.C. 1924. Stampede. Charlie Trieserra steer ridin

resented the Chinese working for lower wages, taking jobs they felt rightfully belonged to others. A series of "head taxes," introduced in 1885 and lasting until 1947, severely limited Chinese immigration. Anti-Asian bias resulted in race riots as early as the 1870s that laid the groundwork for the controversial relocation of Japanese-Canadians to Interior internment camps during World War II.

Many newcomers to British Columbia settled in Vancouver, but others looked to the Interior for relief from unemployment and overcrowding, an escape from various forms of oppression, and a chance for a new beginning. Their new communities created an ethnic patchwork. A group of Norwegians founded Hagensborg near Bella Coola. Italians, attracted by mining and construction jobs, settled in Trail around the turn of the century. Elsewhere in the Interior, colonies of Germans, Swedes, and French-Canadians were among those banding together to start anew.

One major focus of land development was the Okanagan. While some early settlers such as the Oblate Fathers and Thomas Ellis had planted fruit trees and grown market crops, the huge tracts of grazing land established in the 1860s continued to dominate the landscape into the 1890s.

The arrival of Lord and Lady Aberdeen of Scotland in the Okanagan, during

Above: Despite the hard work and long hours required to maintain a living, communities still took time to celebrate their achievements. Cowboy Charlie Trieserra rides a steer at the Williams Lake-Cariboo Stampede in 1924.

Opposite top: Okanagan residents, influenced by their largely British heritage, gathered for a regatta in Kelowna in 1909.

Opposite bottom: Among other recreational pleasures was the dubious sport of paddlewheel racing. Overzealous captains would actually ram each other in their desire to win. The *Rossland, Bonnington,* and *Minto,* docked here at Arrowhead in 1912, worked the Arrow Lakes. It is claimed that the *Rossland* (left) was the fastest in the world.

Top: West Kootenay photographer Mattie Gunterman (left) was often in her own photographs. Here she enjoys an afternoon of skating on "the pond" with friends in Beaton in 1904.

Bottom: A public education system was established in BC in 1872. In the isolated communities of the Interior, fulfilling the mandate was often difficult. Many social activities often centred around the one-room schools.

Opposite: In the East Kootenay region, Radium Hot Springs became a popular recreational destination with the 1922 opening of the Banff-Windermere Highway. These bathers are enjoying waters at Radium Hot Springs in Kootenay National Park, established in 1920.

MISS M SPENCER

Above: "The Grey Fox" was finally captured after robbing a CPR train near Kamloops. Bill Miner, who was reported as polite and apologetic during his robberies, is credited with originating the expression "hands up."

Left: Not all leisured gentry were who they seemed. Posing as the genteel George Edwards, one of America's most wanted stage-coach robbers lived in the Tulameen region near Princeton in the early 1900s.

$500 Reward

The above reward will be paid for the arrest and detention of **WILLIAM (Bill) MINER,** alias Edwards, who escaped from the New Westminster Penitentiary, at New Westminster, British Columbia, on the 8th August, 1907, where he was serving a life sentence for train robbery.

DESCRIPTION:

Age 65 years; 138 pounds; 5 feet 8½ inches; dark complexion; brown eyes; grey hair; slight build; face spotted; tattoo base of left thumb, star and ballet girl right forearm; wrist joint-bones large; moles centre of breast, 1 under left breast, 1 on right shoulder, 1 on left shoulder-blade; discoloration left buttock; scars on left shin, right leg, inside, at knee, 2 on neck.

Communicate with

LT.-COL. A. P. SHERWOOD,
Commissioner Dominion Police,
Ottawa. Canada.

Above: Although the Okanagan underwent a land rush in the early 1900s, cowboys still worked the large cattle ranches that dominated the landscape. In the late 1890s and early 1900s, the economy of the area began to change as land developers bought up the large spreads and subdivided them for smaller orchard plots.

the summer of 1889 is an event that many regard as a turning point. "Up to now but little attention has been devoted to fruit growing as this has been principally a stock-raising country," Lady Aberdeen wrote in *Through Canada with a Kodak,* "but the possibilities shown by the few orchards already planted, point to its ... exceptional advantages for the pursuit of this industry." In 1890 the Aberdeens bought a 200-hectare spread near Kelowna and in 1891, the 5200-hectare Coldstream Ranch near Vernon, dividing it into smaller plots for orchard operations. The Coldstream area was seen as an enclave of well-bred English orchardists pursuing an idyllic agrarian life.

The climate of the Okanagan was indeed appealing, and the CPR's 1892 introduction of regular and reliable rail and paddlewheel service added to the area's attractiveness. In the years before World War I, over 50 companies bought ranches up and down the valley to subdivide and resell as orchards.

Many difficulties faced the pioneer farmers, including high freight costs and crop failures, and their early attempts at commercial success were sometimes disastrous. But hard work paid off, and by 1910, Okanagan fruit was winning prizes at world expositions.

Developers tried to use the vision of the Okanagan as "heaven on earth" to

exploit areas less amenable to cultivation. The lands along the Kootenay and Arrow lakes were also vigorously (and sometimes shamelessly) promoted. To provide proof of mature orchards where none existed, one brochure actually featured photographs of "apple" trees with plump juicy fruit attached to barren branches with string.

Despite the hard work of many of the new settlers, reality often got the better of the vision. Walhachin, in the arid land between Ashcroft and Kamloops on the Thompson River, was one such community.

American C.E. Barnes dreamed of transforming the sagebrush and desert into lush orchards and genteel living, and along with the British Columbia Horticultural Estate, he purchased nearly 2000 hectares in 1906.

The Walhachin developers sold their dream to upper-class English settlers who knew nothing about farming but were attracted by the idea of polo matches, afternoon tea, and fancy dress balls. They purchased planted land for $140 a hectare and four-room houses (with bath) for $1100.

One obvious problem was water. In 1907 the group built a dam on Deadman Lake and constructed a two-metre-wide wooden flume that carried the precious stuff over ravines and hillsides for 30 kilometres to the orchard site. Such tenacity is admirable, but according

Above: Despite the land boom, these workers still brought in the hay at the Hill Ranch near Osoyoos in 1915.

Opposite top: Farmers in the Spallumcheen Valley near Vernon enjoyed the benefits of BC's first reaper in 1899.

Opposite bottom: A continent-wide depression in the early 1890s, crop failures, and marketing problems caused the early orchard industry to falter in the Okanagan. But in 1913 over 20 million pounds of fruit was produced, worth $640,000 to the 30,000 people dependent on the industry. These workers are packing fruit at the Kelowna Farmers Exchange Packing House.

The First Header in B.C.

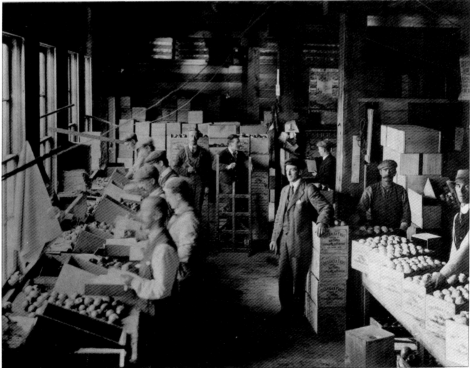

Opposite top: Tobacco was a major crop in the Okanagan until the 1930s. These workers are sorting leaves in a Kelowna cigar factory in 1899.

Opposite bottom: By 1911, nearly 70 percent of BC residents were British by origin, giving a decidedly English flavor to life in the province. Some British immigrants were remittance men, sons of aristocratic families who could not or would not find suitable employment and were sent off to the colonies, supported by a "remittance" from home. Often their ideas of "genteel living" clashed with the harsh wilderness.

Above: In 1907 C.E. Barnes began promoting an ideal English community at Walhachin. Only upper-class English were encouraged to purchase the properties. Their leisured country life would be supported by a lucrative orchard business. Workers here excavate an irrigation ditch in 1910.

to some, it was also the downfall of the community.

So sure were these aristocratic British of their natural superiority that they refused to seek advice from locals. The flume, constructed from green lumber of inconsistent sizes, leaked badly and much of the precious water was wasted. In addition, rather than building the waterway in sections, the men overlapped the crosspieces of the supporting structure, making repair of any single portion of the flume difficult, costly, and cumbersome.

Nonetheless, a hotel was built, the wealthy Marquis of Anglesey created a luxurious estate and invested money, and the fancy dress balls and polo matches proceeded. For a few years the town and orchards thrived.

Then in 1914 World War I broke out. As in other communities in the Interior settled by the British, the men rallied to the call of the motherland. Walhachin's response, however, set a record – of 107 men in the community, 97 finally enlisted, more per capita than any other town in the British Empire.

The casualties were heavy and towards the end of the war a rainstorm destroyed sections of the badly constructed flume. Unable to raise the money to repair the system, the surviving orchardists could only watch as the trees quickly blighted and, like their dreams, died.

About the same time that the privileged English families were uncrating their pianos and fine china at Walhachin, a group of Russian peasants were marching to the West Kootenay area from Saskatchewan. The Doukhobors were not looking for leisured country living, but simply a place where they could live in peace after years of religious persecution.

Since the 17th century, when they broke away from the Russian Orthodox Church, the Doukhobors had been condemned and persecuted in their homeland. In 1898, with the aid of novelist Leo Tolstoy and the Quakers, they settled on communal farms in the area now known as Saskatchewan. Because they were pacifists and believed in the holy spirit present in each individual rather than an external authority, they received special dispensation in Saskatchewan regarding education, land registry, and military service. However, in 1905, this special status was revoked.

In 1908, led by their spiritual leader Peter "the Lordly" Verigin, 6000

Above: A hastily constructed flume, completed in 1910 for a cost of $100,000, transported water over 32 kilometres to the orchard sites. Since trees took at least four years to mature, Walhachin residents were anxious to get their enterprise underway as quickly as possible.

Opposite top: The Walhachin hotel, also completed in 1910, housed orchardists who arrived before their homes were completed, single people, and visitors from England who came for the excellent grouse shooting. Other traditional customs that were maintained in the desert community were formal dress at dinner, afternoon tea, concerts, fancy dress balls, and sporting events such as golf and tennis.

Opposite bottom: In 1898, 7500 Doukhobor peasants immigrated to Saskatchewan from Russia. While breaking the Prairie land, it was not uncommon for women to hitch themselves to the ploughs. When demands by the Saskatchewan government regarding land registry conflicted with Doukhobor beliefs, 6000 Doukhobors trekked to BC in 1908.

Above: This farm near Grand Forks features a large brick farmhouse typical of the Doukhobor communal farms. Led by Peter "the Lordly" Verigin, Russian Doukhobors built 90 farms in the Kootenay-Boundary region, 65 near Castlegar and 25 near Grand Forks.

Opposite top: Most of the farms were built to Verigin's precise specifications, with two large houses providing accommodation for families and individuals. These workers are sharing a communal meal at Brilliant, near Castlegar in the 1920s.

Opposite bottom: The Sons of Freedom were a radical Doukhobor sect who gained notoriety during the 1950s for dramatic protest actions that included nude marches and arson. These children are protesting the incarceration of their Sons of Freedom parents.

Doukhobors trekked to BC in search of "toil and peaceful life." They lived in large brick communal houses and together worked the land, planting orchards and vegetables, and developing industries such as a well-known jam factory at Brilliant.

But their communal dream began to disintegrate in 1924, when Verigin was killed in an alleged bomb attack. During the 1930s, lending institutions foreclosed on the communal lands, and the farms went into receivership.

Farther north, more promises and dreams fuelled settlement of the central Interior. Although fur-trading posts had been established at places like Fort George and Fort St. James as early as 1808,

settlement had not taken hold. The Cariboo Gold Rush had stopped short of Fort George, and although gold rushes in the Omineca Mountains in the 1870s and the 1890s had attracted prospectors, the land was still viewed as inhospitable. Waterways provided the only access to many communities, with sternwheelers connecting isolated settlements. Only the hardiest homesteaders were interested in planting roots and raising families in such country.

A route to the Bulkley Valley region had been established in the 1860s with an attempt by the Collins Overland Telegraph Company to run a cable from San Francisco to Europe through BC, Alaska, and Russia. Begun

Opposite: Another group who didn't find BC "heaven on earth" were the 13,000 Japanese-Canadians exiled from the coast to internment camps in the Interior during World War II. They were given 24 hours' notice to close down homes and businesses, pack personal belongings into two suitcases, and report to registration centres.

Top: The internees were totally responsible for activities within the camps. These children attended kindergarten in Sandon.

Bottom: Often housing consisted of hastily constructed shacks with no insulation. This camp was at Crescent Valley in the West Kootenay's Slocan Valley. Forty-eight hundred internees, the largest number in the Interior, were housed in the Slocan Valley camps.

in 1865, the project was abandoned the following year when a rival company successfully laid a cable across the Atlantic, but not before workers strung wire from New Westminster to Fort Stager, near present-day Hazelton, and they had cleared a rough trail to the Yukon.

The Klondike Gold Rush of 1897 attracted thousands to the area, but most were only passing through. Hazelton and Telegraph Creek became transportation and supply centres, as heads of navigation on the Skeena and Stikine rivers respectively. And in 1902, when the Dominion Telegraph Company took up where the Overland Telegraph Company had left off, the "Telegraph Trail" provided a packtrain route north. But transportation remained a major problem until the first decade of the 20th century.

Then the same railroad fever that had taken over the southern Interior spread to the north. Workers built the Grand Trunk Pacific Railway between 1910 and 1914, connecting Edmonton, Alberta with Prince Rupert on the Pacific coast.

The present-day towns of Smithers, Vanderhoof, Houston, and Burns Lake came into being with the construction of the Grand Trunk Pacific. Their mills

Above: Many of the internees were housed in ghost towns like Sandon, Slocan, and Greenwood, which had been wide-open mining towns less than 50 years before. Despite the hardships, the internees developed communities, clearing land, creating town councils, and holding cultural events. "It was a little Japanese village," one woman recalled. "[Daily life] had nothing to do with the outside world."

Opposite top: In the north, life hadn't changed significantly from the early days of settlement. Fort Fraser, one of the first fur-trading posts in New Caledonia, looked much the same in the 1920s as it did in the early 1800s.

Opposite bottom: An 1865 attempt to establish a telegraph line from San Francisco to Russia through BC could have led to vigorous settlement of the central Interior, but the plan was abandoned in 1866. With its headquarters in New Westminster, the line got as far north as present-day Hazelton.

HARPER'S WEEKLY.
JOURNAL OF CIVILIZATION.

VOL. IX.—No. 450.]   NEW YORK, SATURDAY, AUGUST 12, 1865.   [SINGLE COPIES TEN CENTS. $4.00 PER YEAR IN ADVANCE.

Entered according to Act of Congress, in the Year 1865, by Harper & Brothers, in the Clerk's Office of the District Court for the Southern District of New York.

THE COLLINS OVER-LAND TELEGRAPH.

This immense enterprise, which is to connect America with Europe by the way of California, Behring Strait, and the Amoor River, is being pushed forward with the utmost energy during the present season, under the auspices of the Western Union Telegraph Company. The wires of the California Telegraph Company have during the past winter been extended through Oregon and Washington Territory, as far as New Westminster, the capital of British Columbia, and are now in operation to that point. At New Westminster the Collins Overland Telegraph proper commences, and will extend up Frazer River nearly to its source, and thence nearly parallel with the coast, following the general direction of the valley between the Rocky Mountains and the Coast Range to a point at or near Behring Strait, which will be crossed by a submarine cable. The line will thence extend through the eastern portion of Siberia until it meets the telegraph, now nearly completed by the Russian Government from St. Petersburg to

the mouth of the Amoor River.

The whole work is under the general supervision of Colonel Charles S. Bulkley, Engineer-in-Chief, who will be remembered as the late efficient superintendent of the United States military lines in the Department of the Gulf. Colonel B. is a man of great experience in practical telegraphing, having constructed the first range of wires between Washington and New Orleans, in the year 1847.

The construction of the overland line through the colony of British Columbia is proceeding with great rapidity, considering the mountainous and difficult nature of the country. This division is under the immediate charge of Assistant-Engineer Ed. Conway, late of the United States Military Telegraph. A party, under command of Major F. L. Pope, of Massachusetts, is now engaged in making explorations in the country lying between the head of Frazer River and Behring Strait, in order to determine the most practicable route for the telegraph. Other exploring parties will also be put at work the present season

TERMINAL STATION OF COLLINS'S OVERLAND TELEGRAPH, NEW WESTMINSTER, B. C.—[SKETCHED BY F. L. POPE.]

Above: Hazelton became head of navigation on the Skeena River. The arrival of the paddlewheeler was a major event in communities throughout the Interior. These people await the ship's arrival in Hazelton in the early 1900s. "When we landed at Hazelton, the whole town ... [came] down to meet us," according to Wiggs O'Neill, a crew member and pioneer historian from the Bulkley Valley. "When the ship blew her whistle, everyone waved and cheered and the dogs sat on their hind ends and howled."

Left: When the Overland Telegraph Company crews pulled out of the Hazelton area, they left wire cable and other supplies behind, hoping the construction would resume. Natives built a bridge over the Hagwelgit Canyon on the Bulkley River with some of the leftover material.

Above: In 1902, the Dominion
Telegraph Company completed a line
to the Yukon, using portions of the old
Overland trail. "The Telegraph Trail"
became an important transportation
route connecting northern BC with the
Yukon.

provided ties for the railway and began a logging industry that continues to be an important part of BC's economy.

Land speculators thrived in places like Fort George and Fort St. James. Once work began, they quickly acquired vast tracts of land, buying up timber licences and valuable property along the railway. According to politician John Oliver, "The speculators sometimes get their land for a dollar and a drink and sometimes for a drink without the dollar." In Fort George in 1910, lots sold for $10,000

each. Five years later, the town became Prince George and proclaimed itself "the railway hub of British Columbia" in anticipation of the completion of the Pacific Great Eastern.

The PGE was a joke in the province for many years. Chartered as a private company in 1912 and later taken over by the provincial government, by 1921 the line had only reached Quesnel in the north and Squamish in the south. The public, disgusted with the delays, renamed the beleaguered

Above: The Klondike Gold Rush of 1897 also stimulated interest in BC's north. These miners are hiking over BC's Chilkoot Pass into the Yukon.

Opposite top: While southern Interior towns like Nelson may have been enjoying trolley cars and electric lights, northern life lacked such amenities. The rugged terrain and harsh climate often took their toll. These two men are bringing in the body of a mail carrier in the Babine Mountains in 1910.

Opposite bottom: Packtrains remained an important method of transportation throughout the Interior well into the 20th century. This group is preparing to leave Lillooet in the 1920s.

Jean Caux's Pack Train loading at Harvey Baileys for Babine Lake 1897

Above: One of the Interior's better known packers was Jean "Cataline" Caux (third from left), who transported freight in the Interior for 54 years. Originally from the Spanish-French border region, Cataline began packing in 1858 during the Cariboo Gold Rush and ended his career packing out of Hazelton in 1912. He is pictured loading his packtrain for a trip to Babine Lake in 1897.

Left: This northern packer is "tightening the diamond hitch" on a horse at Fort St. James, probably in the early 1900s. The fort was used as a Hudson's Bay post until the 1930s.

Opposite: Hudson's Bay Company scows transported goods and supplies on the northern lakes. Their arrival was a long-awaited event in isolated communities. This Siwash man demonstrates his good spirits by climbing the mast of a vessel at Fort St. James in 1909.

Above: In 1910, Fort George was a small fur-trading settlement connected to the southern Interior by sternwheelers and wagon roads. Of 100 railway schemes presented during this time, the most significant were the extension of the Grand Trunk Pacific from Edmonton and the construction of the Pacific Great Eastern which would connect Fort George with Vancouver. Land developers anticipated the proposed railways with glee, but the boom didn't materialize.

Left: Born and bred in New Westminster, Richard McBride was the first native son to become a premier of BC. He was also the province's youngest premier. Coming to power in 1903, McBride oversaw a period of development and growth similar to that of Sir James Douglas' during in the 1860s. While Douglas had promoted roadbuilding, McBride encouraged railways.

Opposite: McBride's deals on the GTP included the promise that no Chinese would be hired for construction. However, Chinese workers, such as these photographed in 1909, were employed on the construction of the Canadian Northern Railway, which came south from Edmonton through the Yellowhead pass to Vancouver. The line was completed in 1915.

line "Past God's Endurance," "Please Go Easy," and "Prince George Eventually." It would be another 35 years before the railway was completed from North Vancouver to Prince George, and the central Interior experienced its promised boom.

Farther north, although the Peace River Country saw the establishment of the first fur-trading posts in the early 1800s, subsequent settlement was slow. Some hardy souls, responding to the federal homesteading program, settled the area in the 1890s and early 1900s. And during the 1930s, many farmers from the drought-stricken Prairies moved there. But the problem of transportation and communication remained a difficulty until World War II.

Afraid that the Japanese would attack overland, the American military negotiated with the Canadian government to build an artery connecting isolated airbases and an alternative supply route should their northern bases be shut down. The men charged with creating this route through the wilderness were often raw recruits with little knowledge of road building. An amazing task for the time, the highway had to cross five mountain ranges and over 100 glacier-fed rivers. In some places, five layers of trees and gravel were required to create a solid road-bed on the seven-metre-deep muskeg. When it was finished the road stretched 2430 kilometres through BC's undeveloped northern regions, connect-

ing Dawson Creek to the Yukon and Alaska.

Construction started in March 1942, and the first truck pushed through to Whitehorse in September that same year. However, during the following spring 150 bridges washed out and 240 kilometres of road disappeared in mud and muskeg. Conversion of the road to an all-weather route began. At the height of activity, 17,000 workers, 54 separate contractors, and over 11,000 pieces of equipment valued at 27 million dollars were on the job. The cost of the project totalled a then astronomical 147 million dollars.

In 1952, the John Hart Highway was constructed, connecting Dawson Creek with Prince George, and a north-south road link

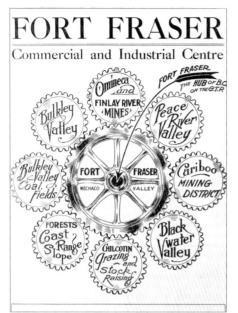

through the Interior was complete.

In the 1950s an unprecedented flurry of road building and resource development took place, attracting more settlers to the Interior's far reaches. In the following decades, hydroelectric projects, the expansion of the PGE (now BC Rail), oil and natural gas discoveries, and tourism have contributed to an evergrowing population.

Today, the boom-bust cycles of a resource-based economy continue; new towns spring up as others die. And while BC's Interior is no longer an uncharted wilderness, the mountains, valleys, and rolling plateaus remain a land of dreams.

Above: Promoters made impossible claims to potential land buyers about prospects in the central Interior. "He who has the courage to break away from old surroundings and make new friends among new surroundings in a new land, will find the right kind of conditions for his happiness and independence ... History will record here in the Nechaco [sic] Valley an endless chain of romance, happiness, and fortune building," claimed *BC Magazine* in 1914.

Opposite top: "The price paid for a Fort Fraser lot is not paid for land alone – it is paid for opportunity," gushed a New Westminster newspaper ad in 1914. The construction of the GTP resulted in the establishment of communities near Prince George such as Vanderhoof, Burns Lake, and Smithers. Here a construction crew works to lay the last metres of track on April 7, 1914 at Fort Fraser.

Opposite bottom: The first Grand Trunk Pacific Train arrived from Winnipeg at the terminus in Prince Rupert on April 9, 1914.

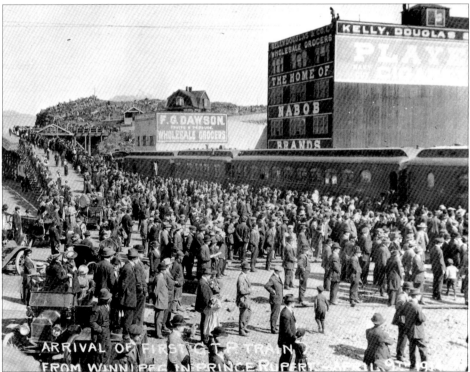

ARRIVAL OF FIRST G.T.P. TRAIN FROM WINNIPEG IN PRINCE RUPERT, APRIL 9TH, 19...

Opposite top: Despite the busy railway activity in the south, settlement of the Peace River country to the north was slow. These Fort St. John farmers could just as easily have been relaxing in front of Finch's store in the 1890s as in the 1930s, when the photograph was taken.

Opposite bottom: Besides offering rich agricultural land for settlement, the Peace River also had jobs in resource development. Horses were commonly used to haul coal to the surface. This team is working underground at the Peace River Coal Mine in Fort St. John.

Top: Alaska Highway construction opened up the northern Interior to large numbers of settlers. Built during World War II, the project attracted thousands of military personnel and civilians to the area. US Army soldiers pitched their tents along the Peace River at Fort St. John, seen in the background of this 1942 photograph.

Bottom: The Alaska Highway, completed in 1942, connected Dawson Creek with the Yukon and Alaska and covered 2430 kilometres. The road was opened to the public in 1946, giving greatly improved access to the northern reaches of BC's Interior.

Meredith Bain Woodward

was born and raised in Vancouver and for 20 years lived in Winlaw in the West Kootenay region. A former travel counsellor for the BC Automobile Association, she has also toured the province many times as a professional actress. She holds a BA and an MFA from UBC and is a past editor of the *Kootenay Business Journal.* She currently lives in Vancouver.